AMAZING AIRPLANES BOOK FOR CURIOUS KIDS

Dive into the Fascinating World of Aviation, Legendary Pilots, and Thrilling Flight Mysteries!

TIM LYLANI

Copyright © 2024 TIM LYLANI

All rights reserved.

TIM LYLANI

TABLE OF CONTENTS

INTRODUCTION 5

Dreaming of the Skies 9

The Wright Brothers Take Off 13

Breaking Boundaries 17

The Sky's First African American Pilot 25

The Daring Atlantic Flight 17

The Maverick Aviator 31

The Birth of the Jumbo Jet 37

The Supersonic Wonder 41

Secrets in the Sky 45

The First Jet Engine 49

The Eyes in the Sky 53

The Flying Car Dream 57

Aerial Knight of World War I 63

Heroes in the Sky 67

The Unsung Heroes of the Skies 71

A Plane That Changed History 77

A Spy Plane Ahead of Its Time 81

The Miracle on the Hudson 87

Flight 19 and the Bermuda Triangle 91

Survival Against All Odds 95

The Disappearance of MH370 99

The Ghost Planes of Aviation History 103

Flying Around the World 107

What Keeps a Plane in the Sky? 113

Inside the Cockpit 117

The Hidden Heroes 123

From Parts to the Sky 127

Why Do Airplanes Have Black Boxes? 131

The Next Big Thing 137

The Role of Aviation in Space Exploration 141

CONCLUSION 145

INTRODUCTION

From the moment the Wright brothers took their first flight to the latest missions exploring the skies and beyond, airplanes have been a source of wonder, adventure, and innovation. In this book, you'll discover incredible stories, fascinating facts, and the science behind flight. Whether you dream of soaring like a bird, becoming a pilot, or exploring outer space, this book is your ticket to learning how flight changed the world and is still shaping the future.

Buckle up as we take you on a journey through history, science, and technology. You'll meet brave pilots, incredible inventors, and even the planes that have made the impossible possible. You'll learn how airplanes stay in the sky, what it takes to build a plane, and how aviation is helping us reach for the stars. From the mystery of missing planes to the dream of flying cars, this book will make you see the world of aviation in a whole new way.

So, are you ready to take off? Let's get started! The adventure is about to begin.

PART ONE

TIM LYLANI

Dreaming of the Skies

Have you ever stared at a bird soaring high in the sky and thought, "Wow, I wish I could do that!"? Well, guess what? Humans have been dreaming of flying for thousands of years! Long before airplanes, jet engines, or even hot air balloons, people imagined what it would be like to spread their arms, take off, and feel the wind beneath their feet.

One of the oldest stories about flight comes from Greek mythology. There was a boy named Icarus who lived with his father, Daedalus, on a beautiful island. But here's the twist: they weren't there on vacation—they were trapped! So, Daedalus came up with a daring plan. He made wings out of feathers and wax (yes, wax!) so they could escape by flying away.

"Stick close to me," Daedalus warned Icarus. "Don't fly too high or too low."

But Icarus, feeling the thrill of the wind in his hair, soared higher and higher. The sun melted the wax in his wings, and—uh-oh—he tumbled into the sea! It was a big lesson in following directions, but the story also showed how much humans longed to fly.

Fast forward a few thousand years, and we meet one of the most curious and creative minds in history: Leonardo da Vinci. Leonardo wasn't just a painter (ever heard of the Mona Lisa?); he was also a scientist and inventor who loved thinking about flight. He watched birds, sketched their wings, and came up with crazy-cool ideas for flying machines.

One of his inventions was called the "ornithopter." It had flapping wings that looked like a bird's and was powered by pedals, kind of like a bicycle. Did it work? Not quite. But it was a step closer to figuring out the secrets of flight!

Leonardo even studied parachutes. He believed if you had a triangular frame covered with cloth, you could float gently to the ground. And guess what? Hundreds of years later, someone tested his design, and it worked! Leonardo was ahead of his time.

From ancient myths to brilliant inventions, the dream of flying never faded. People were determined to figure it out, no matter how wild their ideas seemed. The sky wasn't just a place for birds—it was a frontier waiting to be conquered.

It's incredible to think that something humans could only imagine for centuries has become such a big part of our world. All it took was courage, creativity, and the belief that no dream is too high to reach.

The Wright Brothers Take Off

Imagine a world without airplanes—no trips across oceans, no soaring above the clouds, and no speedy mail deliveries. Hard to picture, right? But over a hundred years ago, there were no airplanes at all. The idea of flying seemed impossible. That's where two brothers, Orville and Wilbur Wright, came in.

Orville and Wilbur grew up in Dayton, Ohio. They weren't just regular kids; they were tinkerers. They loved to take things apart and figure out how they worked. One day, their dad brought home a helicopter-like toy made of bamboo and paper. It was powered by a rubber band, and when the boys wound it up, it flew into the air. That little helicopter lit a spark in their imaginations.

As they got older, the brothers started their own bicycle shop. But bikes weren't enough for them—they wanted to tackle something bigger: the dream of flight. Inspired by birds and kite-flying, they began studying everything they could about aerodynamics, which is the science of how things fly.

The Wright brothers didn't just want to glide through the air like some inventors of their time. They wanted a powered machine that could lift off, stay in the air, and be controlled by the pilot.

Years of trial and error followed. Their first attempts didn't go so well. Some planes barely left the ground; others crashed spectacularly. But they didn't give up. Each failure taught them something new. They experimented with designs, built their own wind tunnel, and even created a lightweight engine for their plane.

Finally, on December 17, 1903, everything changed. They traveled to Kitty Hawk, North Carolina, a place with steady winds and soft sand for landing. The brothers flipped a coin to decide who would pilot the first flight. Orville won.

With Wilbur running alongside, Orville climbed into the wooden flyer. The engine roared to life, and the plane wobbled down the rail. Then, like magic, it lifted off the ground. It stayed in the air for just 12 seconds and flew 120 feet—about the length of two school buses. But those 12 seconds were enough to prove that humans could fly.

The brothers didn't stop there. They kept improving their designs, making planes that could fly longer and farther. Soon, their invention caught the world's attention, and the age of flight began.

Their journey shows how big ideas can turn into real achievements with creativity and hard work. The skies, once unreachable, opened up to endless possibilities thanks to Orville and Wilbur's determination.

The Daring Atlantic Flight

In 1927, the world was buzzing with excitement about a challenge that seemed almost impossible: flying non-stop across the Atlantic Ocean. Many pilots had tried and failed, but a young, determined aviator named Charles Lindbergh believed he could do it. With courage, skill, and a little bit of luck, he set out to prove it could be done.

Charles grew up in Minnesota, where he spent his childhood fascinated by machines. He was a farm boy with a knack for fixing engines and a dream of taking to the skies. As he got older, his love for aviation grew, and he became a skilled pilot, flying mail planes across the country.

In those days, crossing the Atlantic by plane was incredibly dangerous. Planes weren't very advanced, and bad weather or running out of fuel could easily spell disaster. But the idea of a solo flight from New York to Paris captured Charles's imagination.

To take on the challenge, Charles needed a special airplane. He worked with engineers to create the Spirit of St. Louis, a single-engine plane designed specifically for the journey. It wasn't built for comfort—there was only one cramped seat, no windows to look forward, and barely enough room for food and water. Every inch of the plane was designed to save weight and carry as much fuel as possible.

On May 20, 1927, Charles took off from Roosevelt Field in New York. The plane was so heavy with fuel that it barely cleared the trees at the end of the runway. His journey had begun, and there was no turning back.

The flight wasn't easy. Over the Atlantic Ocean, there were no landmarks, no maps, and no way to call for help. Charles had to rely on his compass and his instincts to navigate. He battled freezing winds, dense fog, and the crushing loneliness of flying alone for hours on end. To stay awake during the 33-hour flight, he splashed cold water on his face and pinched his arms.

Finally, after flying more than 3,600 miles, Charles spotted the lights of Paris. Crowds had gathered at Le Bourget Field to witness his landing, cheering wildly as he touched down. Charles Lindbergh had done it! He became the first person to fly solo and non-stop across the Atlantic Ocean, and the world hailed him as a hero.

His daring flight wasn't just about winning a prize—it inspired people to believe in the power of aviation. Charles showed that with determination and bravery, even the greatest challenges could be conquered. His journey across the Atlantic opened the skies to new possibilities and paved the way for the future of flight.

Breaking Boundaries

What if someone told you that flying across the world wasn't just for men in leather jackets and goggles? Amelia Earhart set out to prove that adventure and bravery knew no gender—and she did it with courage, confidence, and a love for soaring through the skies!

Amelia was born in Kansas in 1897, and even as a little girl, she loved exploring. She wasn't afraid to climb trees, race down hills on her sled, or try daring stunts. Amelia believed that girls could do anything boys could do, and she carried that belief with her into adulthood.

Her fascination with flying began one day at an airshow. A pilot swooped down close to the crowd, and Amelia felt something she couldn't ignore: a spark of inspiration. From that moment on, she knew she wanted to fly.

Amelia worked odd jobs, from photographer to truck driver, to save enough money for flying lessons. When she finally stepped into a cockpit for the first time, she felt like she belonged among the clouds. She learned fast, and soon, Amelia was breaking records left and right.

In 1928, she became the first woman to fly across the Atlantic Ocean as a passenger. But that wasn't enough for Amelia. She wanted to pilot the plane herself. Four years later, she did just that, becoming the first woman to fly solo across the Atlantic. The flight was dangerous—she faced icy winds, a leaky gas tank, and a malfunctioning altimeter. But after 15 hours in the air, she landed safely in Ireland, greeted by cheering crowds.

Amelia didn't stop there. She broke records for speed and distance, inspiring people everywhere. But what really captured the world's attention was her boldest dream: to fly all the way around the globe.

In 1937, Amelia and her navigator, Fred Noonan, set out on their historic journey. They traveled thousands of miles, making stops in South America, Africa, and Asia. But as they approached the most challenging leg of their trip—crossing the Pacific Ocean—Amelia's plane vanished.

To this day, no one knows exactly what happened. Some believe her plane ran out of fuel; others think she landed on an uninhabited island. Her disappearance remains one of the greatest mysteries in aviation history.

Even though her final journey ended in tragedy, Amelia's legacy lives on. She showed the world that women could achieve incredible things and inspired generations to dream big, take risks, and never back down from a challenge.

Her story isn't just about flying; it's about courage, determination, and blazing a trail for others to follow. Amelia Earhart didn't just break boundaries—she soared above them.

The Sky's First African American Pilot

Have you ever dreamed of doing something no one around you thought you could do? That's exactly what Bessie Coleman did. She didn't just follow her dreams—she soared above them, proving to the world that anything is possible with enough courage and determination.

Bessie Coleman was born in 1892 in a small town in Texas. Life wasn't easy for her family. They were poor, and Bessie often had to help out by picking cotton or doing laundry. But she didn't let hard times stop her. Bessie was curious, full of energy, and always ready to learn.

One thing she loved to do was read about daring adventures. Stories about airplanes and the new age of flight fascinated her. But back then, there were no African American women pilots. Flying seemed like an impossible dream for someone like Bessie.

Bessie refused to let prejudice stand in her way. She knew she'd have to work extra hard to achieve her dream. She moved to Chicago as a young woman and worked as a manicurist, saving every penny she could. However, when she tried to enroll in flight schools in the United States, she faced rejection after rejection. No one would train her because of her race and gender.

Then Bessie had an idea—if she couldn't learn to fly in the U.S., she'd go somewhere else. Inspired by the stories she'd heard about France, where women pilots were gaining recognition, Bessie decided to cross the ocean to pursue her dream.

In 1920, Bessie sailed to France, even though she didn't speak the language. She was determined to succeed. French flight schools welcomed her with open arms, and she learned to fly on open-cockpit planes. These weren't the sleek jets you see today; they were rickety biplanes that shook and rattled in the wind. But Bessie loved every second of it.

After months of training, she earned her pilot's license, becoming the first African American woman—and the first Native American woman—to do so. She didn't stop there. Bessie returned to the U.S. as a hero, dazzling audiences with breathtaking airshows.

At her performances, she performed loops, spins, and daring dives. But Bessie had a bigger mission. She wanted to inspire others to reach for the skies, no matter their background. She refused to perform for segregated audiences and insisted that her shows welcome everyone.

Bessie's story didn't have a long ending—she tragically passed away at just 34 in a flying accident. But in her short life, she broke barriers, paved the way for future aviators, and showed the world the power of believing in your dreams.

Bessie Coleman's courage and determination changed aviation forever. She proved that the sky isn't just the limit—it's where dreams can soar the highest.

AMAZING AIRPLANES BOOK FOR CURIOUS KIDS

TIM LYLANI

The Maverick Aviator

A young man with big dreams and bold ideas once decided that the sky wasn't high enough for his ambition. Howard Hughes wasn't your typical pilot. He wasn't just interested in flying planes; he wanted to build the fastest, biggest, and most incredible aircraft anyone had ever seen. And he did—all while living a life as wild as his inventions!

Howard grew up in Texas, surrounded by gadgets and machines. He loved figuring out how things worked, whether it was a car engine or a camera. His curiosity only grew when he discovered airplanes. Flying wasn't just a hobby for Howard—it became his obsession.

But Howard wasn't content with just flying planes; he wanted to make them better. He poured his energy into designing aircraft that could go faster and farther than anyone thought possible. One of his most famous creations was the H-1 Racer, a sleek, shiny plane that looked like it belonged in a futuristic movie. In 1935, Howard climbed into the cockpit of the H-1 and set a world speed record, racing through the air at an astonishing 352 miles per hour.

Howard didn't stop at breaking records. He dreamed of building the largest plane in the world. During World War II, he designed the Hercules, a massive wooden aircraft that people nicknamed the "Spruce Goose." The plane was so huge that many doubted it would ever fly. But Howard believed in his creation. In 1947, he piloted the Hercules on its first—and only—flight. It soared over the water for about a mile, proving that even the craziest dreams could come true.

Apart from being a brilliant inventor, Howard was also an adventurer. He loved pushing boundaries and taking risks. In 1938, he flew around the world in just 91 hours, setting a new record and showing that air travel could connect the globe faster than ever before.

However, Howard's life wasn't all smooth skies. He was known for being eccentric and often kept to himself, especially later in life. Despite his quirks, his contributions to aviation were unmatched. He showed the world that being a little different could lead to extraordinary achievements.

Howard Hughes wasn't afraid to dream big, break the rules, and take flight—literally and figuratively. His legacy lives on in the planes he built, the records he shattered, and the inspiration he left for anyone daring enough to aim for the skies.

PART TWO

TIM LYLANI

The Birth of the Jumbo Jet

One sunny day in 1968, something amazing happened in the world of airplanes. The sky was about to get a lot more crowded—and a lot more exciting. A brand-new type of plane was about to take its first flight, and it was so big it looked like a flying skyscraper! This was the Boeing 747, also known as the "Jumbo Jet."

Before the 747, planes were much smaller. If you wanted to fly from one country to another, you'd have to sit in a cramped seat and share a tiny space with other passengers. Flying across the world was an adventure, but it could also be uncomfortable and expensive.

The Boeing 747 changed everything. Designed by an amazing team of engineers at Boeing, it was the first airplane big enough to carry hundreds of people at once. It had two giant engines on each wing, a nose that could lift up to let people walk straight into the plane, and a special upper deck that felt like a whole new world. When it first flew, people couldn't believe how massive it was. It was like a giant bird soaring through the sky!

This incredible plane made flying so much more accessible. Imagine hopping on a plane with your family and traveling to faraway places like Europe or Asia—without breaking the bank! The 747 made that possible, as airlines could now fit more passengers on each flight, making tickets cheaper and trips faster.

But the 747 wasn't just big—it was also fast. The plane could zoom through the sky at incredible speeds, getting passengers from one place to another in record time. And, because it could carry so many people, it changed the way airlines thought about flying. It became the go-to plane for long flights, like those across the ocean, where you could relax, sleep, and even enjoy a meal in the sky.

Airlines all over the world rushed to get their hands on the Jumbo Jet, and soon, it was flying everywhere—from bustling cities to remote islands. The Boeing 747 wasn't just a plane—it was a whole new way of traveling.

Look up when you see a huge plane soaring through the sky, and you might just be looking at a piece of history! The Boeing 747 made air travel faster, easier, and a lot more fun. Thanks to this amazing Jumbo Jet, the world got a little bit smaller, and the adventure of flying got a whole lot bigger!

The Supersonic Wonder

In the world of airplanes, there's one that's faster than a speeding bullet and cooler than most superheroes. It's called Concorde, and it's not just any plane—it's the fastest passenger plane ever built!

Concorde first took to the skies in 1969, and it wasn't like anything anyone had ever seen before. While other planes cruised along at speeds that seemed pretty fast, Concorde was like a rocket in the sky, zooming at more than twice the speed of sound. That's over 1,350 miles per hour! If you were flying in Concorde, you could get from New York to London in just a few hours. That's way faster than most jets and a whole lot faster than driving across a country.

What made Concorde even cooler was its sleek, pointy nose. The nose would tilt down during takeoff and landing so pilots could see better, but during flight, it looked like something out of a science fiction movie—a jet with a nose like an arrow cutting through the sky. Inside, it wasn't like a regular airplane either. Passengers could sit in comfortable seats, enjoy delicious food, and feel like they were traveling in style. Everything about Concorde was designed to make the journey as smooth and exciting as possible, even while flying at unbelievable speeds.

But speed came with a price. Because the Concorde was so fast, it could create a loud sonic boom—a huge sound that happens when something breaks the sound barrier. While passengers loved the speed, people on the ground sometimes didn't like the noise. In fact, Concorde could only fly over certain areas to avoid disturbing people with its loud roar. That didn't stop people from thinking Concorde was amazing, though.

Unfortunately, Concorde's flying days ended in 2003, after more than 30 years in the sky. It was a sad day for aviation fans everywhere, but Concorde's legacy still lives on. It showed the world that flying could be more than just getting from one place to another—it could be an incredible experience, like riding a lightning bolt through the sky.

Concorde was more than just a plane; it was a symbol of human achievement. It proved that when people dream big, anything is possible. Even though Concorde doesn't fly anymore, its place in history will never be forgotten. It was the supersonic wonder that changed the way we think about travel and showed the world how far we can go when we push the limits of what's possible!

Secrets in the Sky

What if there were planes that could sneak through the sky like invisible ninjas? That's exactly what stealth planes are! They're some of the coolest and most mysterious aircraft ever built, designed to fly undetected right past radar systems. But how does something as big as a plane stay hidden?

Stealth planes don't use magic, even though it might seem like they do. Instead, they use super-smart science. Radars work by sending out signals that bounce off objects and come back, kind of like an echo. If the radar "hears" the echo, it knows something is out there. But stealth planes are built in a way that makes radar signals slip right past them, so they don't bounce back. It's like being a master of disguise—but in the air!

One of the coolest stealth planes is the F-117 Nighthawk. This plane looks nothing like a regular airplane. It has sharp angles and flat surfaces instead of the usual smooth, rounded shapes. These sharp edges help scatter radar signals in all directions, making the plane practically invisible to detection systems. To top it off, the Nighthawk is coated with special materials that absorb radar waves instead of reflecting them. Talk about high-tech camouflage!

But stealth technology isn't just about dodging radar. These planes are also designed to make as little noise as possible so they can sneak up quietly. They even hide their engines in clever ways to make sure heat-seeking systems can't spot them. It's like the plane is wearing a super suit that hides everything from sound to heat to radar signals.

Stealth planes have been used in many important missions, often flying over areas where regular planes would be easily spotted. They've been used to gather information, deliver supplies, and even protect people, all while staying under the radar—literally!

What's amazing about stealth technology is how it keeps evolving. Engineers are always working on new ways to make planes even more invisible and efficient. Stealth technology doesn't just make planes harder to see; it also shows how creative and determined humans can be when solving problems.

Stealth planes are proof that the sky is full of secrets—and that with enough innovation, humans can achieve incredible things!

TIM LYLANI

The First Jet Engine

Long ago, airplanes had propellers that spun around and around to push them through the sky. They were fast but not fast enough for the big dreams of inventors and pilots. That's when someone came up with a genius idea: the jet engine. This invention turned planes into speed machines, changing air travel forever!

The story starts with a brilliant man named Frank Whittle. He wasn't just any inventor—he loved thinking about how to make planes faster and better. In the 1930s, while other people were working on improving propeller engines, Frank was imagining a whole new way to fly. He believed that air could be sucked into an engine, mixed with fuel, and burned to create a powerful blast of hot air that would shoot out the back of the engine, pushing the plane forward.

Think of it like blowing up a balloon and letting it go. The air rushing out makes the balloon zoom around the room. That's how a jet engine works—except way more powerful and way more controlled!

In 1941, Frank's invention was finally ready to take flight. The first jet-powered plane, called the Gloster E.28/39, roared down the runway and soared into the sky. It was a huge moment in history! While it didn't break any speed records right away, it proved that jet engines could work. Pilots and engineers knew this was just the beginning of something amazing.

Jet engines made planes faster than anyone had ever imagined. Suddenly, people could travel across countries and even oceans in just hours. The world felt smaller, and the possibilities felt endless. For fighter planes in World War II, jet engines gave an edge in speed and power. After the war, passenger planes with jet engines made air travel popular for everyone—not just for pilots or the wealthy.

Today, almost every airplane you see in the sky uses a jet engine. From tiny jets to giant airliners, they all owe their speed and power to that first invention. Without the jet engine, we might still be flying in slow, noisy propeller planes!

The first jet engine wasn't just a machine; it was a leap into the future. It showed that sometimes, the most daring ideas can change the world—one incredible flight at a time.

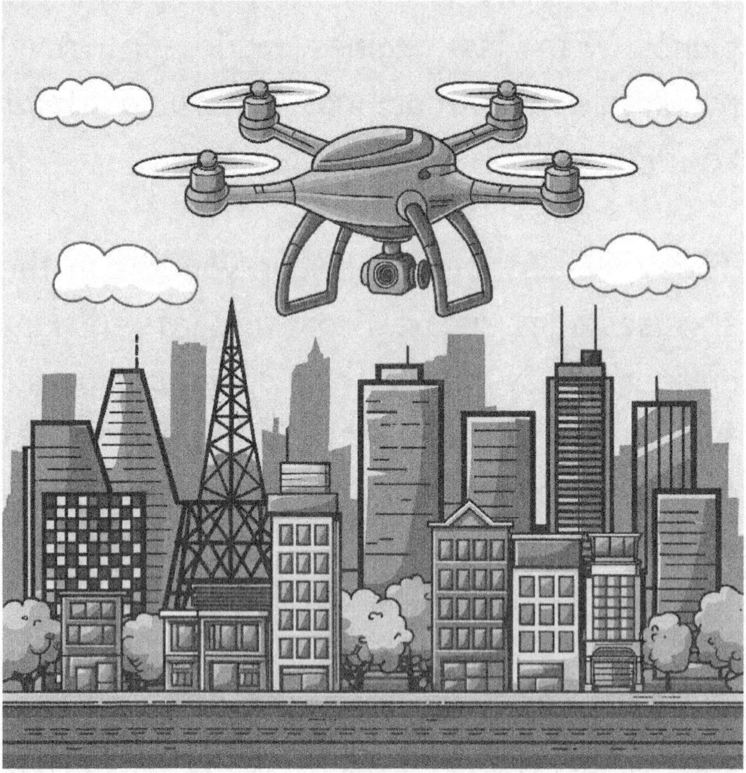

The Eyes in the Sky

Meet drones: the coolest little flying machines that are taking over the skies! They don't need a pilot sitting inside because they can be controlled from the ground—or even programmed to fly on their own. It's like having a robot with wings! Drones have so many jobs, from delivering packages to saving lives and even exploring places humans can't go.

Drones started off as high-tech gadgets for big jobs, like helping scientists and soldiers. Over time, they became smaller, smarter, and much easier to use. Now, you can find drones buzzing around for all kinds of reasons. Some are no bigger than your hand, while others are huge and powerful. But no matter the size, drones are always ready for action.

One of their coolest uses is delivery. Imagine ordering something online and having a drone bring it to your doorstep! Companies are already testing ways to make this happen. The drone picks up a package, flies over traffic and obstacles, and gently lowers it down to your home. It's faster than any truck and way more exciting.

Drones are also heroes in emergencies. They can fly into dangerous places where it's too risky for humans to go. For example, during wildfires, drones help firefighters by showing where the flames are spreading. In search-and-rescue missions, drones use cameras and sensors to find people who are lost or stranded. They can even carry small supplies like water or medical kits to people in need.

And let's not forget about exploration. Drones are like fearless adventurers, flying high above mountains, deep into jungles, or over vast oceans. They help scientists study animals, map forests, and even explore volcanoes! Some have gone to places humans could never reach, like the surface of Mars, where NASA's drone helicopter Ingenuity is buzzing around and gathering amazing data.

Of course, drones are also just plain fun. People use them to take incredible photos and videos, race them like high-speed cars, or just watch them zip around the sky. But behind the fun is some serious science. Every drone is packed with clever technology, like GPS, to know where it's going and cameras to see what's around.

Drones are changing the world one flight at a time. They're not just eyes in the sky—they're helpers, explorers, and sometimes even lifesavers. Wherever they go, drones prove that when humans and technology work together, the sky is no longer the limit.

The Flying Car Dream

What if cars could fly over traffic, zooming through the skies like something out of a sci-fi movie? That dream might not be as far off as you think! Inventors and engineers around the world are working hard to make flying cars a reality. They want to build vehicles that can drive on roads and take off into the air when needed. Pretty awesome, right?

The idea of flying cars has been around for over a century. Even back in the 1920s, people imagined cars with wings gliding through city skies. But it turns out that building a car that can also fly is a lot trickier than it sounds. It needs to be light enough to take off, strong enough to handle the air, and safe enough for everyone inside—and outside!

One of the first big attempts at a flying car was the Aerocar in the 1950s. It looked like a regular car, but with wings, you could attach when you wanted to fly. Cool, but not very practical—imagine parking that thing! Since then, inventors have come up with all kinds of designs, from cars with propellers to futuristic ones that look like drones.

Today, companies are getting closer than ever to creating real flying cars. Some vehicles are powered by electricity, making them quieter and better for the environment. Others are designed to take off straight up, like a helicopter, so they don't need long runways. These flying cars could be used to avoid traffic jams, travel quickly between cities, or even make rescue missions faster in emergencies.

Flying cars could change the way cities look, too. Roads might become less crowded, and buildings could have special landing pads on rooftops. Instead of stoplights, we could have air-traffic lights! But for all this to happen, there's still a lot to figure out, like how to make flying cars affordable, safe, and easy to use.

Some flying car prototypes are already being tested. There are videos of them soaring through the sky, looking like something out of a superhero movie. It's not hard to imagine a future where flying cars are as normal as buses or bikes.

The flying car dream is more than just cool—it's a symbol of what humans can achieve when they dare to think big. Whether it's zipping above traffic or taking short trips through the clouds, flying cars might soon make the dream of the open road an adventure in the open sky!

AMAZING AIRPLANES BOOK FOR CURIOUS KIDS

PART THREE

WARBIRDS AND THEIR STORIES

Aerial Knight of World War I

During World War I, the skies weren't just for birds—they became a brand-new battlefield. High above the trenches, pilots zoomed around in biplanes, engaging in thrilling aerial battles called "dogfights." And no pilot was more famous—or more feared—than Manfred von Richthofen, known to the world as the Red Baron.

The Red Baron wasn't called that because he liked red jellybeans or wore a red cape. His nickname came from his bright red airplane, a Fokker triplane that stood out in the sky like a firework. Most pilots tried to blend in to stay safe, but not the Red Baron. He wanted everyone to know when he was coming. Bold, right?

Manfred von Richthofen didn't start out as a pilot. At first, he was a cavalry officer, riding horses into battle. But when airplanes became the newest tool of war, he was curious and signed up to fly. It turns out he had a natural talent for it. He wasn't just good—he was unbeatable.

The Red Baron quickly became a legend, with over 80 victories in aerial combat. Pilots would tell tales of his incredible skill and sharp instincts. He could outmaneuver almost anyone, making him a nightmare for enemy planes. His red triplane became a symbol of fear in the sky.

But the Red Baron wasn't just known for his flying skills—he was also admired for his sense of honor. He followed a "code of chivalry," treating his enemies with respect. Even in the chaos of war, he acted like a true knight of the air.

Dogfights weren't just about speed or firepower—they were about strategy and bravery. Planes in World War I were made of wood and fabric, which meant they weren't very strong. Pilots had to rely on their wits to stay ahead of their opponents. It was like an intense game of tag, except in the air and with real danger.

Manfred's time as the Red Baron ended in 1918 when he was shot down in battle. Even though he was on the opposing side, his enemies honored him with a respectful burial, recognizing his skill and bravery. His legend has lived in inspiring books, movies, and even video games.

The Red Baron's story isn't just about being the best—it's about daring to soar higher, fight smarter, and stay true to a code of respect, even in the toughest of times. Up in the clouds, he became more than a pilot. He became a symbol of courage and the spirit of adventure.

Heroes in the Sky

In the summer of 1940, a fierce battle was fought—but not on the ground. It was in the skies above Britain where brave pilots faced one of the most challenging fights of World War II. This was the Battle of Britain, and it became one of the most important air battles in history.

At the time, Britain was in serious trouble. Germany, led by Adolf Hitler, wanted to invade the country. But to do that, they needed to defeat the Royal Air Force (RAF). So, they sent waves of planes called the Luftwaffe to bomb cities, airfields, and factories. The skies were filled with roaring engines, dark smoke, and the constant sound of explosions.

The RAF pilots were outnumbered, but they refused to give up. They flew Spitfires and Hurricanes—small, fast fighter planes that were perfect for dogfights. These pilots were young, skilled, and incredibly brave. They had to zoom into battle, often facing dozens of enemy planes at once.

The pilots nicknamed the German bombers "Heinkels" and "Stukas," and they became experts at taking them down. Each time the RAF shot down an enemy plane, it was like a small victory in a much larger war. The pilots worked tirelessly, sometimes flying multiple missions in a single day, knowing that their efforts were protecting millions of people below.

But the Battle of Britain wasn't just about machines and dogfights. It was also about teamwork. The RAF used something called radar, which was a brand-new invention at the time. Radar stations along the coast could detect incoming enemy planes, giving the pilots enough time to prepare for battle. It was like having eyes that could see hundreds of miles away!

The people on the ground were heroes, too. Women worked as radar operators, plotting the positions of enemy planes on large maps. Mechanics worked around the clock to fix damaged planes, sending them back into the fight as quickly as possible. Even regular citizens helped, putting out fires and keeping spirits high despite the danger.

After months of intense fighting, the RAF pilots had done the impossible: they stopped the German invasion. Historians say it was the first major defeat for Germany in World War II. Winston Churchill, Britain's leader at the time, called the pilots "The Few" and said their courage would never be forgotten.

The Battle of Britain showed the world what determination and bravery could achieve. These pilots weren't just defending their country—they were defending the idea of freedom itself. They became legends, proving that even when the odds are against you, courage can turn the tide of history.

The Unsung Heroes of the Skies

During World War II, something incredible happened. While men were off fighting in the war, millions of women stepped up to take on jobs that had never been open to them before. They worked in factories, built airplanes, and even flew them! These women didn't just help—they showed the world what they could do.

Rosie the Riveter became the symbol of these hardworking women. She wasn't a real person but a character in posters and ads, flexing her muscles and saying, "We can do it!" She inspired women to join the effort, and boy, did they! They learned how to rivet, weld, and assemble airplanes in record time. Imagine a giant jigsaw puzzle, but instead of small pieces, you're putting together wings, engines, and cockpits.

In factories across the United States, women became experts at building planes like the B-17 bomber and the P-51 Mustang. These machines were vital for the war, and thanks to the women's speed and precision, the military had thousands of planes ready to go. The factories buzzed with energy as women proved they could handle these tough jobs just as well as anyone else.

But building planes wasn't the only way women contributed. Many joined the Women Airforce Service Pilots (WASP). These pilots didn't fly in combat, but they had crucial missions, like testing planes, towing targets for training exercises, and delivering aircraft to military bases. Flying was no easy task, and these women had to be as brave as they were skilled.

One of the most famous WASP pilots was Jacqueline Cochran, who also happened to be one of the fastest fliers of her time. She trained hundreds of women to fly military planes and even broke several flying records herself. Talk about leading by example!

The WASP pilots faced danger every day. Planes could break down, the weather could turn nasty, and they had to fly without the advanced technology pilots use today. Yet, they handled it all with courage and determination. They were true pioneers, proving that women could excel in the skies.

After the war ended, many women were expected to go back to their old lives, but their impact couldn't be erased. They had shown the world that women could do anything they set their minds to—whether it was building powerful planes or soaring through the clouds.

Rosie the Riveter and the women of aviation didn't just help win the war. They broke barriers, opened doors, and inspired generations to dream bigger. Their story is a high-flying adventure of courage, teamwork, and unstoppable spirit!

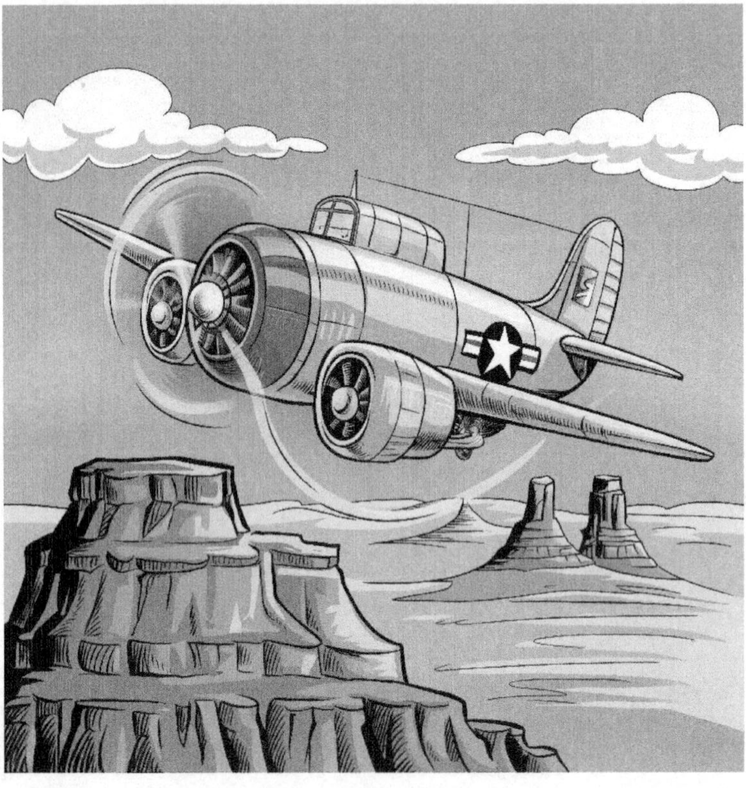

A Plane That Changed History

In the middle of World War II, a shiny silver airplane took to the skies, carrying a mission that would change the course of history forever. Its name was the Enola Gay, and it was no ordinary plane. It became famous—and controversial—for carrying the first atomic bomb ever used in war.

The Enola Gay was a B-29 Superfortress, a massive plane with four powerful engines. It was built to carry heavy loads and fly long distances, which made it perfect for its special mission. The plane was named after the mother of its pilot, Colonel Paul Tibbets, who led the daring operation.

The mission began in the early morning hours of August 6, 1945. The Enola Gay took off from a tiny island in the Pacific Ocean, carrying a bomb nicknamed "Little Boy." But this wasn't just any bomb—it was an atomic bomb, the most powerful weapon ever created at the time. It was so secret and so new that even some of the crew didn't fully understand what they were carrying.

The target was the city of Hiroshima in Japan. The goal was to force Japan to surrender and end the war. As the Enola Gay approached its destination, the crew prepared for the drop. At exactly 8:15 a.m., Little Boy was released from the plane, falling silently through the sky.

Then, in a flash of light brighter than a thousand suns, the bomb exploded. The power was immense, creating a massive shockwave and a towering mushroom cloud. The destruction was devastating, and the event left an impact that would be felt across the world.

The crew of the Enola Gay watched the explosion from a safe distance, stunned by what they saw. The mission was successful, but it also brought immense loss and raised questions about the use of such a powerful weapon. Just a few days later, another atomic bomb was dropped on Nagasaki, leading to Japan's surrender and the end of World War II.

The story of the Enola Gay is a complicated one. It played a key role in ending a terrible war, but it also showed how destructive and dangerous atomic bombs could be. This one plane carried not just a bomb but the weight of history itself.

Today, the Enola Gay is on display in a museum, a powerful symbol of the moment when science and war intersected, changing the world forever. It's a story of innovation, courage, and the impact of decisions—decisions that shaped the future of humanity.

A Spy Plane Ahead of Its Time

Meet the SR-71 Blackbird, a plane so fast and so cool it seemed like something out of a science fiction movie. But this wasn't just a futuristic design—it was real, and it was one of the most legendary spy planes ever built.

The Blackbird was created during the Cold War, a time when countries were trying to outsmart each other with technology and information. The United States needed a plane that could fly higher and faster than anything else, one that could sneak over enemy territory and gather secrets without getting caught. That's where the Blackbird came in.

This jet was built to be unstoppable. Its sleek black body wasn't just for looks—it helped absorb radar signals, making it hard to detect. It could fly more than three times the speed of sound, reaching speeds of over 2,200 miles per hour! At that speed, it could cross the entire United States in about an hour.

The Blackbird didn't just rely on speed. It flew so high, almost at the edge of space, that no enemy plane or missile could reach it. Pilots needed special suits, almost like astronaut gear, to survive the extreme conditions at 85,000 feet in the air.

What made the Blackbird even more amazing were its secret missions. It wasn't armed with weapons; instead, it carried high-tech cameras and sensors to spy on enemy activity. Its cameras were so powerful that from miles above, they could take clear pictures of objects as small as a license plate!

Despite its incredible abilities, flying the Blackbird wasn't easy. Its skin got so hot from the friction of flying at supersonic speeds that it had to be made of titanium. Even then, the plane expanded during flight, so it had tiny gaps in its panels when on the ground. Engineers had to design special fuel that wouldn't leak during takeoff but could handle the intense heat mid-flight.

The pilots who flew the Blackbird were some of the best in the world. They trained for years to handle the unique challenges of this one-of-a-kind plane. Flying at such speeds wasn't just about skill—it also took nerves of steel.

The SR-71 Blackbird was retired in the 1990s, but its legend lives on. No other plane has matched its combination of speed, height, and stealth. It wasn't just a plane—it was a masterpiece of engineering, a secret agent in the sky, and proof that humans could dream big and make it fly.

PART FOUR

"AVIATION ADVENTURES AND MYSTERIES"

TIM LYLANI

The Miracle on the Hudson

On January 15, 2009, a plane flying over New York City found itself in big trouble. A loud thud shook the aircraft. A flock of birds had knocked out two engines! Now, the plane was floating in the sky with nothing to keep it moving forward. The pilot, Captain Chesley "Sully" Sullenberger, had a tough decision to make: he needed to land the plane fast—and safely.

Sully was an experienced pilot, but this was a situation no one could prepare for. With the plane losing power, Sully realized he couldn't make it to any nearby airport. The only option left? He decided to land the plane on the Hudson River, right in the heart of New York City.

The people aboard the plane, 155 passengers and crew, didn't know it yet, but they were about to witness something amazing. Sully calmly told the crew, "We're going to be in the Hudson." In a situation where many people might panic, Sully stayed cool and focused. He needed to make sure everyone was safe.

With no engines to help steer, Sully had to glide the plane over buildings and traffic, looking for a spot on the water. As the plane got closer to the river, he guided it down smoothly, using all his training to bring it in safely. The plane hit the water with a gentle splash—amazing for a plane that was hundreds of tons heavy. It stayed mostly intact, and everyone on board stayed calm.

The rescue teams worked quickly. Boats rushed to the scene, and within minutes, all passengers were safely aboard the rescue ships. Not a single life was lost. It wasn't just a landing; it was a miracle.

The whole world watched as Sully became a hero. He had saved everyone aboard the plane with his quick thinking, steady hands, and years of experience. The "Miracle on the Hudson," as it was called, showed us all that sometimes, the right person in the right moment can do something truly amazing. Captain Sully didn't just land a plane—he gave the passengers a second chance at life.

TIM LYLANI

Flight 19 and the Bermuda Triangle

On December 5, 1945, five Navy bombers took off for a routine training mission over the Atlantic Ocean. The pilots, part of a squadron known as Flight 19, were experienced and ready for the challenge. They were supposed to fly out, do some practice runs, and return home safely. But that day, something went horribly wrong.

As they flew deeper into the sky, the weather started changing. Dark clouds covered the sun, and soon, the pilots couldn't see the landmarks they needed to stay on course. Lieutenant Charles Taylor, the lead pilot, radioed into air traffic control, saying he was lost and couldn't figure out where he was. Despite being an experienced pilot, he couldn't find his way back. The other pilots on Flight 19 were equally confused. They had all made mistakes in navigation and couldn't agree on which way to go.

The strange part? Flight 19 wasn't the only plane that disappeared that day. After the bombers were lost, a rescue plane went out to find them. But it too vanished, as if swallowed by the ocean. No wreckage, no signs of the planes, and no survivors. The only thing left behind were radio signals that seemed to come from nowhere and disappear just as quickly.

What happened to Flight 19? It's one of the biggest mysteries connected to the Bermuda Triangle, an area in the Atlantic Ocean where many planes and ships have disappeared over the years. Some people think the Bermuda Triangle is cursed, while others believe there's something strange about the magnetic fields in the area that messes with navigational instruments. Others suggest wild theories like aliens or underwater creatures taking the planes.

No one really knows the truth, and the mystery of Flight 19 has puzzled experts for decades. Even with modern technology like sonar, satellite images, and underwater robots, no one has ever found the planes that disappeared that day.

While the Bermuda Triangle continues to be a place of mystery and wonder, it also shows how much there still is to learn about the world around us—especially when it comes to the deep, vast ocean where secrets may still be waiting to be discovered.

Survival Against All Odds

High up in the Andes Mountains, a group of young athletes were about to face the most terrifying challenge of their lives. It all started on October 13, 1972, when a plane carrying Uruguayan rugby players and their friends crashed in the middle of the mountains. The crash was bad—there were no roads, no food, and no way to call for help. They were completely stranded in a place so remote nobody even knew they were missing.

At first, the survivors tried to stay positive. They used the plane wreckage as shelter and hoped for a rescue to arrive soon. But days turned into weeks, and no one came. They didn't have enough food or water, and the freezing mountain weather made everything harder. The survivors knew that the longer they waited, the worse their chances of survival became.

One of the hardest moments came when the food ran out. With no more supplies, the group had to think carefully and work together to find new ways to survive. They learned to be resourceful and relied on each other's strength to get through the tough times.

Weeks passed, and the survivors never gave up. Even though their situation seemed hopeless, they kept trying to find a way out. Finally, after over two months, two of the survivors decided to go on foot and find help. They climbed mountains, crossed dangerous rivers, and walked for miles—doing whatever it took to survive.

Finally, after an exhausting journey, they found help! A rescue team arrived to save the rest of the group. Against all odds, 16 survivors made it out of the mountains, their spirits stronger than ever.

The story of the Andes survivors is one of the most incredible tales of survival in history. Even though everything seemed impossible, they kept fighting, staying alive, and never losing hope. It shows that when faced with even the darkest times, the human spirit can shine bright and push through the toughest challenges.

TIM LYLANI

The Disappearance of MH370

On March 8, 2014, something mysterious happened in the sky. Malaysia Airlines Flight MH370, a big passenger plane, took off from Kuala Lumpur, Malaysia, heading for Beijing, China. The passengers were excited to reach their destinations, but no one had any idea that this flight would become one of the biggest mysteries in aviation history.

Just a few hours after takeoff, something strange occurred. The plane lost contact with air traffic control. It disappeared from the radar as if it had vanished into thin air. The pilots didn't send any distress signals, and the flight path seemed to change unexpectedly.

What happened next was even more puzzling. The plane didn't crash immediately—it seemed to keep flying for hours, changing direction. Despite all the technology available, no one could figure out where the plane went. MH370 was never found.

The search for the missing plane went on for years. Thousands of people worked together, using submarines, drones, and other tools to search the vast ocean where the plane might have crashed. They found a few pieces of the plane on remote islands in the Indian Ocean, but the main wreckage still hasn't been found.

Why did the plane disappear? Was it a technical failure? A mistake? Or something else entirely? The mystery of MH370 still hasn't been solved. Some people believe the answers might be hidden deep underwater, while others wonder if we will ever really know what happened.

The disappearance of Flight MH370 is one of the most mysterious events in aviation history. Even today, it raises questions about what happens when something goes wrong in the sky and how we might be able to prevent such disappearances in the future. One thing is for sure: the story of MH370 has captured the world's attention, leaving many wondering what really happened to the plane that seemed to vanish without a trace.

TIM LYLANI

The Ghost Planes of Aviation History

In the world of aviation, there are some strange stories that leave people scratching their heads. One of the creepiest involves ghost planes—aircraft that flew with no one at the controls! These planes became famous because they took off and flew without any pilots or crew on board, and they kept going as if they had a mind of their own.

One of the most famous ghost plane stories is about a DC-3 aircraft that was flying from the United States to the Caribbean back in 1947. After it took off, something went wrong. The plane's crew disappeared, and the plane kept flying. It wasn't responding to radio calls, and air traffic controllers had no idea who was piloting it. For hours, the DC-3 flew on autopilot, heading out over the ocean with no one in charge. The mystery wasn't solved until the plane eventually ran out of fuel and crashed. It was like the plane had a ghostly life of its own, continuing its journey even without anyone at the controls.

There's also the story of the L-8 blimp that became a ghost in the sky. In 1942, the blimp was sent on a mission to patrol the Pacific Ocean. But when it was found, there was no one inside! The blimp had been flying on its own for hours. The crew was missing, and the blimp had simply drifted on the wind. It became a real-life mystery for authorities to solve. How did it keep flying with no one in the cockpit?

Then there's the famous story of the Fly-by-wire systems, which are autopilots that can control a plane's movements without a human pilot. But there have been a few eerie situations where the plane kept flying on its own, even after something went wrong, and it didn't respond to commands from air traffic control. It was as if the plane was just... moving by itself!

These 'ghost plane' stories are among the strangest and eeriest moments in aviation history. While modern technology and autopilot systems have made air travel safer than ever, these mysterious flights show that the sky sometimes holds secrets we may never fully understand. It's hard not to wonder what happens when planes fly with no one in charge. Where do they go? And what keeps them flying, all alone in the sky? That's one mystery that might remain unsolved."

Flying Around the World

Flying around the world is a dream for many, but for a few brave pilots, it became a reality! These daring adventurers took to the skies, flying their planes across oceans, deserts, and mountains to complete an epic journey—circumnavigating the entire globe!

One of the most famous globe-trotting flights happened in 1924 when four American pilots set off in Army Air Service planes to fly around the world. They didn't have the technology we have today, like GPS or satellites, so they had to rely on old maps and their gut instincts. It wasn't easy! They flew through storms, faced mechanical problems, and even had to deal with engine failures. But after 175 days and over 26,000 miles, they completed their journey and made history. Their adventure showed just how brave and determined pilots can be!

In 1937, another incredible journey happened when Amelia Earhart, one of the most famous pilots in history, tried to fly around the world. She was already a hero for being the first woman to fly solo across the Atlantic Ocean. But her final journey, flying with her navigator, Fred Noonan, would take her to new heights. Unfortunately, Amelia's plane disappeared somewhere over the Pacific Ocean, and to this day, no one knows exactly what happened to her. But her courage and spirit still inspire people around the world to chase their own dreams of flying!

Then there was the team of Steve Fossett, an adventurer who made history by being the first person to fly solo around the world in a hot air balloon in 2002. Steve's journey took him over 20,000 miles and lasted more than two weeks. It was an incredible feat of bravery and determination. He didn't just fly in a plane—he soared through the sky in a balloon, powered only by the wind and his skill!

In 2016, Randy and Carol set off on a daring mission to fly around the world in a tiny plane, the Piper Navajo. Their adventure was filled with challenges, from crazy weather to unpredictable landings, but they stayed strong and completed their flight. They flew over the oceans, crossed deserts, and landed in countries they'd only dreamed of visiting. Their journey showed that no matter how difficult the road (or sky!) is, you can always make it if you have determination and a love for adventure!

These brave pilots are part of a long tradition of those who push the limits of what's possible, all in the name of adventure. Flying around the world isn't easy—it requires skill, courage, and a lot of planning. But those who set out on these amazing journeys showed us just how big and exciting the world can be when you're up in the sky, flying free.

AMAZING AIRPLANES BOOK FOR CURIOUS KIDS

PART FIVE

"HOW PLANES WORK"

What Keeps a Plane in the Sky?

Ever wonder how a giant airplane packed with people, luggage, and snacks can stay up in the sky without falling down? It's all thanks to a clever thing called aerodynamics. That's the science behind how air moves around objects, and it plays a huge part in keeping planes up where they belong—up high in the clouds!

The main secret to keeping a plane in the sky is something called lift. Lift is a force that pushes the plane upwards, and it happens when the air pressure above the plane's wings is lower than the air pressure below the wings. But how does that work? Let's break it down!

The wings of an airplane are designed to be curved on top and flat on the bottom. When the plane speeds down the runway and starts flying, air moves over and under the wings. Because the top of the wing is curved, the air above it has to travel faster than the air below it. Faster air means lower pressure, and that creates a suction effect that pulls the plane upwards—this is lift in action! Meanwhile, the higher pressure under the wings pushes up as well, giving the plane an extra boost.

But that's not all! To keep the plane flying smoothly, the pilots need to use thrust and drag. Thrust is the forward force that makes the plane move, and it's created by the engines. The engines work by pushing air out at the back of the plane, which makes the plane move forward. As the plane moves forward, the wings keep creating lift, helping it stay in the sky.

However, the plane also has to fight against drag. Drag is the resistance from the air that tries to slow the plane down. Pilots have to work with the engines and wings to make sure the plane keeps enough speed to overcome drag and keep flying high.

Another part of the plane that helps with flying is its tail. The tail helps to keep the plane steady and helps it move in the right direction. It's like the rudder on a boat—it keeps the plane on course so it doesn't start spinning around!

So, in a nutshell, a plane stays in the sky because of the clever design of its wings, the speed at which it travels, and the teamwork between lift, thrust, and drag. It's kind of like a dance between the airplane and the air, where everything has to work together to keep the plane flying safely.

TIM LYLANI

When you're on a plane, look out the window and see how all those parts work together to keep you soaring through the clouds!

Inside the Cockpit

Ever wonder what it's like to sit in the front of an airplane, with the entire world below you and all those buttons and gadgets around you? That's where the pilots sit, and it's called the cockpit! It's like the control center of the whole plane. So, what do pilots do to keep the plane flying smoothly? Let's take a fun peek inside the cockpit and explore all the amazing tools they use!

When you walk into the cockpit, the first thing you'll notice is all the buttons, levers, and screens. It's like a spaceship in there, but it's all built to help the pilots fly the plane safely. There are hundreds of instruments, but don't worry! We'll break it down into the coolest ones.

One of the most important tools in the cockpit is the yoke or control stick. This is what the pilots use to steer the plane left or right and to tilt it up or down. It's kind of like the steering wheel of a car but a lot more powerful! When the pilot moves the yoke, it changes the plane's elevator (the part of the plane's tail) to tilt the plane up or down and the ailerons (the flaps on the wings) to roll the plane left or right.

Next, let's talk about the throttle. The throttle is like the gas pedal for the plane—it controls how much power the engines use. When the pilot pushes the throttle forward, the plane speeds up. If they pull it back, the engines slow down, and the plane can start to descend. The faster the engines go, the higher the plane can climb!

One of the most important displays in the cockpit is the altimeter. This gadget shows the pilots how high the plane is flying, so they know if they're above the clouds or cruising at their perfect altitude. It's like the airplane's altitude meter, and it helps pilots know when to climb, cruise, or descend safely.

Then, there's the attitude indicator. No, it's not for tracking the pilot's mood! This tool shows whether the plane is flying straight or if it's tilting up, down, left, or right. Pilots use it to make sure the plane stays balanced, especially when flying through clouds or at night.

There's also a special screen called the navigation display that helps pilots know exactly where they are flying. It's like a GPS for planes. It shows the path the plane is taking, nearby airports, and any weather problems up ahead. This way, the pilots can fly with confidence, knowing exactly where they're going.

And let's not forget about the radar! Pilots use radar to "see" what's around them, even when they can't see it with their own eyes. The radar sends out signals to detect weather conditions like thunderstorms and even other planes nearby. It's like the plane's own set of superhero X-ray vision!

Of course, every cockpit has lots of other tools and gauges, like the fuel gauge, which tells pilots how much gas is left, and the landing gear lever, which lowers the wheels when it's time to land.

The cockpit is where all the magic happens. Pilots work with all these instruments to keep the plane flying safely through the skies. They work as a team with air traffic controllers, other pilots, and even the airplane itself, making sure everything runs smoothly.

Next time you board a plane, you'll know that behind all the windows and seats, there's a crew of skilled pilots sitting in their cockpit, making sure you get to your destination safely. They've got their hands on the controls, keeping an eye on all the instruments and guiding the plane through the clouds with confidence!

TIM LYLANI

The Hidden Heroes

When you're flying through the skies, there's a whole team of people making sure everything runs smoothly. These people work behind the scenes, but they're some of the most important in the world of aviation. They're called air traffic controllers.

You might wonder what air traffic controllers actually do. They guide planes safely through the sky, making sure they don't get too close to each other. It's kind of like a big game of chess but with planes and super high stakes! Every plane has to be in the right place at the right time.

Air traffic controllers use lots of cool technology to help them do their job. They sit in big rooms with tons of screens, showing them where all the planes are flying. They even have special radar systems that let them see planes from miles away, like having eyes in the sky! If a plane is getting too close to another one, the controllers step in and give directions to keep them safe. They might say something like, "Climb to 10,000 feet" or "Turn left to avoid traffic."

These controllers don't just work with planes that are taking off or landing. They also help planes that are flying way up high in the sky, cruising from one city to another or even crossing oceans. They're always talking to pilots, giving them updates, and helping them navigate through different weather conditions or busy airspace.

And they never stop working. Whether it's the middle of the day or the middle of the night, air traffic controllers are on the job, keeping the skies safe. Their job is non-stop and requires a lot of focus because every plane must stay in its own space.

Whenever you're flying, think about the air traffic controllers who are working hard behind the scenes. They're the unsung heroes who make sure every flight gets where it needs to go safely.

TIM LYLANI

From Parts to the Sky

Have you ever wondered how airplanes are made? It's not as simple as putting a few pieces together. Building an airplane is a huge team effort that takes a lot of time, tools, and skills. Let's take a look behind the scenes at how those big, shiny jets come to life!

The first step in building an airplane starts with designing it. Engineers and designers sketch out all the parts and figure out how everything should fit together. They use super cool computers to create blueprints that show exactly how the plane should look and work. It's like drawing the world's most complicated and awesome puzzle!

Once the design is ready, it's time to make the parts. Airplanes are made up of hundreds of different pieces—wings, engines, the body (called the fuselage), and the tail. Each part is built separately, often by different teams of people. Some parts are made of super strong metals, while others are made of lightweight materials to keep the plane from getting too heavy.

After the parts are made, they're brought together in a giant assembly line. Picture a massive, open space with huge tools and machines. The parts of the airplane start to come together one by one. First, they attach the wings to the main body. Then, they add the tail and connect the engines. It's like building a giant LEGO set, but much, much bigger—and with real metal!

Next, the plane gets its engines. This is one of the most exciting parts! Engines are like the heart of the airplane. They're huge and powerful, and they help the plane take off and fly high in the sky. The engines are carefully placed, making sure they're perfectly connected so they can work properly during flight.

Now comes the test phase. Just because the plane looks ready doesn't mean it's time to fly yet! Engineers and pilots check every part of the plane to make sure it works. They test the brakes, the engines, and even the buttons in the cockpit to make sure everything is safe. They also do lots of tests to see how the plane reacts to wind and different weather conditions. It's like when you test out a new bike to make sure the brakes work before going on a ride!

Finally, after all the testing, the airplane is ready to fly. The plane gets its final touches—like painting on its colors and logos—and it's all set to go. Once the crew has finished everything, the airplane is ready to take passengers all over the world.

Building an airplane is a huge project that involves a lot of people working together. From engineers and designers to mechanics and pilots, everyone plays an important role. In the future, when you see an airplane soaring through the sky, you'll understand the effort and teamwork that make it possible!

Why Do Airplanes Have Black Boxes?

When you hear the words "black box," you might think of something mysterious or secret. But did you know that airplanes actually have these black boxes, and they play a huge role in keeping air travel safe?

Don't be fooled by the name—black boxes aren't really black at all! They're usually bright orange or red, making them easy to spot if they ever need to be found. But why are they so important, and what do they do?

The main job of a black box is to record everything happening on a flight. It's like a super-smart notebook that never forgets anything! There are two types of black boxes: the Flight Data Recorder (FDR) and the Cockpit Voice Recorder (CVR). Both of them are packed with technology that helps figure out what happened during a flight, especially if something goes wrong.

The Flight Data Recorder (FDR) keeps track of the plane's important information. It records things like the speed of the plane, the altitude (how high it is), and even how fast the pilots are moving the controls. The FDR also records whether the engines are working properly and how the plane's systems are functioning. It's like a high-tech diary that tells exactly what was happening to the plane during the flight.

The Cockpit Voice Recorder (CVR) is a little different. It captures all the sounds in the cockpit—the place where the pilots sit. This includes conversations between the pilots, radio communications with air traffic controllers, and any other sounds like alarms or warning signals. It's like recording a podcast of what's happening in the cockpit!

You might be wondering why do we need these black boxes? Well, sometimes things go wrong, and there are accidents or unexplained problems during a flight. The black box helps investigators understand what happened. By listening to the sounds and looking at the data, experts can figure out how the plane was flying and what the pilots were doing. This helps them solve mysteries and figure out ways to make flying even safer in the future.

Black boxes are incredibly strong! They're built to survive even the worst conditions— like huge crashes or fires. They can withstand extreme temperatures and high pressure, which means they can often be found even after a plane accident. Once they're found, the information inside is carefully analyzed by aviation experts.

These little boxes might look simple, but they help solve big mysteries. Thanks to black boxes, investigators can piece together the clues and make flying safer for everyone. So, while they might be hidden away inside the plane, these little orange boxes are always looking out for us in the sky!

PART SIX
THE FUTURE OF FLIGHT

TIM LYLANI

The Next Big Thing

What do you think of when you hear the word "electric"? Maybe you think of the phone you charge every night or the electric cars zooming down the street. Well, guess what? Electric planes might be the next big thing in the world of flying!

For many years, airplanes have used jet fuel—a kind of gas that powers the engines and helps planes fly through the sky. But just like how electric cars are starting to replace gas-powered cars, scientists and engineers are dreaming up a future where electric planes could replace traditional fuel-powered ones. Sounds cool, right?

So, how would electric planes work? Well, instead of burning fuel to create power, electric planes would use batteries—just like the ones in your phone or video game controller, but way bigger and more powerful! These batteries would send electricity to the plane's motors, giving it the power to soar through the sky without using traditional fuel.

You might be wondering: "Can batteries really give a plane enough power to fly?" That's a great question! Right now, electric planes are still in the testing stage, and they're mostly used for short flights. These planes aren't ready to carry hundreds of passengers across oceans just yet, but they're making progress! Engineers are working hard to make bigger batteries that can hold more energy, which means electric planes could eventually fly much longer distances.

Why is this so exciting? There are some really awesome benefits to flying on electric planes. For one, they're better for the environment. Traditional planes burn fuel, which creates pollution and adds to climate change. Electric planes, on the other hand, produce less pollution. If more planes were electric, it could help reduce the amount of harmful gases in the air!

Electric planes could also be quieter than regular planes. If you've ever been on an airplane, you know that it can get pretty noisy. However, with electric engines, there would be less noise, which would make flying more peaceful for passengers and people on the ground.

Plus, electric planes might be cheaper to run. Electricity costs less than jet fuel, so airlines could save money on energy. That could mean cheaper tickets for you and me!

Right now, there are already a few electric planes in the air, but they're small and used for testing. Some companies are designing small passenger planes that could fly people to nearby cities in the future. One day, though, we might see big electric jets flying across the country or even around the world. Who knows? Electric planes could be the future of air travel!

As scientists and engineers continue to improve electric technology, we might just be on the edge of a new era in flying. The future of air travel could be cleaner, quieter, and faster—and it might just be

The Role of Aviation in Space Exploration

Flying into space might sound like something from a science fiction movie, but it's becoming more and more like reality every day! The world of aviation—the technology behind airplanes—has helped us do some pretty amazing things, and now it's playing a key role in helping us explore space. If we want to send humans to Mars, aviation technology is going to be super important!

Right now, when we think about flying, we usually picture planes soaring through the sky. But to get to Mars, a planet millions of miles away, airplanes aren't enough. That's where spacecraft come in. These are like super-powered airplanes designed to fly out of Earth's atmosphere and into the stars. The same principles that make airplanes work here on Earth are also used to design these spacecraft that travel through space!

So, how does aviation help us explore other planets? The answer lies in aerodynamics—the science of how things move through the air. When airplanes fly, they use aerodynamics to push against the air around them, creating lift that helps them rise into the sky. But in space, there's no air, so aircraft have to work a little differently. Spacecraft, like the Mars rovers that explore the Martian surface, use rockets to launch off Earth and travel through space.

A big part of this journey involves space shuttles and space capsules—special flying machines that can carry astronauts to space and back safely. These spacecraft are designed to be able to handle the heat and pressure of space travel. But here's where aviation tech really shines: flight controls, the kind pilots use to fly airplanes, are used in space shuttles, too. Astronauts inside these spacecraft use similar tools and controls to steer their missions, making sure everything goes smoothly.

Now, let's talk about Mars. The Red Planet is a huge challenge for explorers because it has a very thin atmosphere, which makes flying there trickier. But aviation is still playing a huge part in our exploration of Mars! For example, NASA sent a helicopter called Ingenuity to Mars as part of a mission to help us explore the planet. Ingenuity is a small, lightweight helicopter that can fly through Mars' thin air to take pictures and gather important information. This mission is helping us learn more about how we could explore Mars and other planets using aviation tech.

In the future, as we work toward sending humans to Mars, aviation will be more important than ever. We'll need airplanes and helicopters designed for Mars' atmosphere. We might even see flying machines that can take astronauts on exploration missions across the planet, helping us learn more about Mars and other space destinations.

Aviation technology is also helping with space stations like the International Space Station (ISS), which orbits Earth. These stations help astronauts train and prepare for missions to other planets. The technology used to send these spacecraft into orbit and to Mars will keep improving, opening up even more possibilities for the future of human space exploration!

Who knows what the future holds? One day, we might be able to hop onto a spaceship and fly to Mars just like we do with airplanes today! With aviation technology leading the way, the sky's the limit—or should we say, the stars are the limit?

CONCLUSION

As we've learned, aviation isn't just about flying—it's about pushing the boundaries of what's possible. From the first flight of the Wright brothers to the cutting-edge technology of electric planes, the world of flight is constantly evolving, inspiring new generations to dream big. Whether it's solving mysteries in the sky, designing futuristic flying cars, or helping astronauts explore the stars, aviation continues to shape the way we live, travel, and even think about the future.

Who knows? Maybe one day, you'll be the one to design the next great airplane or even travel to Mars! The sky isn't the limit—it's just the beginning. So keep dreaming, keep learning, and remember, in the world of aviation, anything is possible.

The adventure doesn't end here. Keep your curiosity soaring, and who knows where your next flight will take you!

Printed in Great Britain
by Amazon